Why Boys Don

Their Mothers

How to Impact and Change

the Future of Boys Ages 5-13

with Difficult Behavioral

Problems

Table of Contents

Introduction

In 2019, the United States of America was home for 2 to 17 million children who all had something in common. They were diagnosed with ADHD, a behavior problem, anxiety, depression or a combination of all four. The key word that should have caught your attention is the word "diagnosed". Millions of others go undiagnosed and that's where the greater problem lies. Lack of awareness leads to lack of treatment. Lack of treatment leads to kids growing up and becoming adults who never received help. These untreated adults make babies. And so goes the cycle.

The issue with mental health is the stigma surrounding it. I'll share a quick story with you. One day a shirtless little boy was walking down the street with cuts on his back in an unfamiliar neighborhood. No one recognized who this kid was, and they began wondering, "where the heck are his parents". His cuts were not bleeding too bad, but you can tell that this kid has endured some pain - pain that most people would rather wish to avoid. Your reaction, along with everyone else watching this poor little guy, is to cringe at the sight. You heart is swallowed with pain and pity imagining what that must have felt like for him. Next thing you know, you see a middle-aged woman stop the boy, ask him if he's doing okay and if he needs to see a doctor for his wounds. He responds by saying, "what wounds?". She says, "these scars on your back look really bad, you should get them treated so it doesn't worsen. If you let this fester, it's going to be really hard for you when you're older buddy. I'm concerned. Doesn't it hurt?". Then the boy says, "well yes, but my mom said these scars are normal and they'll heal themselves if I leave them alone." The end.

Oops sorry, I left out a small part. Actually, this story isn't about a boy who had scars on his back. It's a story about a boy who has scars on his brain, heart, and thoughts. This is a story about a boy with discipline, mental and behavioral health issues. Except, there is no woman who came to warn him because she can't physically see the scars on his mind. And no, you are not cringing at the sight of this boy because on the surface, he looks fine. Yes, it's true that his mother decides to ignore his behavior hoping it's just a phase. What occurs inside our minds is always going to receive less care and attention due to the fact that it's hard for humans to address problems that cannot be seen or touched. However, we all know the power of our minds far outweighs our physical capabilities. That power is what makes us the greatest species on planet Earth. But it's time we recognize that our brains, hearts, and thoughts are not indestructible just because they're protected by the shells, we call...our bodies.

These behavioral disorders occur in early childhood between ages 2 to 11 and boys are more likely than girls to have a mental, behavioral, or developmental disorder. What does this mean for you as a mother, father, grandparent, sibling, teacher, or caregiver? It means that if you're taking care of a child who shows any of these problems, your job will be harder. This book is dedicated to empowering and training women, men, professionals, providers, families and more. You see, this book is raw, it's real, and it gives information based on experience and research of someone who has worked in the field of mental health with the same types of children you're here to learn about. I've healed those untouchable scars for these young ones with infield therapy and treatment. Boys who have behavioral, disciplinary, and mental health issues need your action to get the help and treatment they deserve. Congratulations for taking that action today and making the right decision to be the best parent you possibly could be.

Now, because you're here, I hope you don't expect this book not to challenge you as those who take action are ultimately held to a different standard in this world. You should be done hearing weak advice like "stay strong", "don't give up", or "nothing is wrong". If you're a mother, you are the strongest creature there is and there's no debating that. Because you're strong, it's time we graduate you to the next level. This book is meant to give information, principles, and actions to reshape your son's behaviors. Expect the unfiltered truth about what gets results. Some of it is unorthodox. Some of it, you've heard before. Some of it is going to make you uncomfortable. But, none of it is purposeless. If you're a teacher, replace the word "parent" with "teacher" in this book. If you're a mental health professional, replace the words "your son" with "your client". Regardless of the titles of the relationship, there are only two types of characters mentioned - adults and boys under the age of 13. Replace the terms to best fit your circumstances. These are the same tactics, methods, mindsets, and strategies I've used to take a boy who was defiant with no regard for self-control to an outstanding little man who could carry his own and who respected the authority figures and peers around him.

Who am I? Oh, I'm nothing special, I can tell you that. Everything I do, you can do as well. But allow me to introduce myself. My name is Victor Moody. As stated earlier, I've worked in the field of child mental and behavioral health. I launched Kidshapers in 2020 to provide parents the best-in-class solutions to child behavior management. Instead of spending countless hour researching and expending your energy to find results, you have us to depend on. You'll learn more about me and the company as the book goes on. In short, anyone who deals with children is considered a Kidshaper. You have the power to impact this child and shape their thoughts, habits, and behaviors for the rest of their lives. None of you lack importance because you are the determining factor that drastically forecasts the future of the entire human race.

Let me share some common responses, excuses and reasons that are made on a daily basis that really gets me frustrated. "Every school in urban areas has no resources". "I lack the time and the money". "That does not work for my son". "Am I a bad parent?". "What's the worst thing you've seen a child do?". "I don't know where he learned that from". The list goes on and on. Did you know that one study estimated a need for 30,000 child and adolescent psychiatrists but discovered that only 6,300 were in practice? On top of that, teachers and staff in schools lack training on trauma-informed care, interventions, understanding children on a deeper level and managing behaviors. In other words, they're screaming for help.

The reason why all of these statements and questions, good and bad, frustrates me is because the only people who suffer from all of this "lack" is the children; the boys who need the help and treatment. It takes awareness, action, and discipline to make change and this book gives you all three. By the end of this, you should be annoyed with the fact that your son listens to you too much rather than too little. If you're able to breathe and feel confident about your ability to guide your son's behavior and improve your relationship with him, then he can trust you as his leader. You'll be healthier, stronger, brighter and so will he.

Most of the terms, strategies and methods presented in this book are based from a wide range of experiences, mentorship and evidence-based practices. However, the goal is not to bombard you with all the technical terms of child mental health and behavior modification. The mission is not for you to be able to debate with the most esteemed psychologists in the world. That's another book. We're not going to waste your time and fill your head with scientific mumbo jumbo (yeah, I said it, mumbo jumbo) that you don't understand. Our job is to take that mumbo jumbo, combine it with experience, and turn into a usable resource for everyday people like you and me to understand. One of the best lines in the history of mankind is, "what's the point of knowing something if you can't explain it in simple terms". It's about time you were the recipient of some quick and easy steps to heal a relationship that should have been healed a long time ago. Sit up, not back. Listen up. Open your ears, your mind and your heart to a better world. Let's close the door to your past life and welcome the new you and the new him.

Chapter 1: Staying in Control When He's Out of Control

Whose Fault Is It?

Do any of these inner thoughts and questions sound utterly familiar. "Is it me? What makes my son so different? Did I do something wrong? Where did he learn that? Is he hurting or does he simply enjoy hurting others? I give him love. Why doesn't he understand? He must have gotten these behaviors from those damn kids at his school. Who do I take him to for help? What will my friends and family think of me? I really just don't know what to do. This is embarrassing. I'm tired. What in the world did I get myself into? I love my kid but..."

If you've had these thoughts, you may be looking for someone or something to blame which is rather understandable. Your brain is a three-quarters of a pound, search and destroy tactician for problems. It's always searching for problems, trying to understand why they exist, and what to do to stop your world from blowing to shreds. You constantly try to piece together where things went wrong. The bottom line is that seeking the root cause of the problem can be extremely subjective at times. Parents are stressed spending hours a day thinking about the problems with their son so much that they have no energy to figure out ways to solve it. They're not headed towards the desired result of improvement. They're stagnant.

This is why I despise any professional who gives personalized advice without actually seeing the child in action. An office is a controlled environment and listening to stories based on people's memories is a surefire way to perceive the wrong information. Just ask the criminal justice system. In a country where innocent people have been accused and convicted crimes due to "eyewitness" testimonies, we still have people who have yet to be exonerated. If a person losing their freedom due to someone else's mistake is not enough proof that memories are terribly defective, then what is? Not to mention, people including myself have blind spots that we refuse to confront or are too unaware of to notice. Memory can be warped and transformed over time or it can even happen as fast as one minute. Sure, a diagnosis can be given based on repeated occurrences. However, if memory is faulty due to human nature, how can we trust someone to help our relationships if it leads to inaccurate declarations. For example, a common example is one person can see the child's behaviors and declare them as a defiant whereas the other sees him as attention seeking. He's not defiant. That's a smokescreen. He simply uses defiant behaviors to receive more attention. Now, every time the parent sees defiance, they try to have a plan to dissolve it when, in fact, the best plan of action would be to do nothing and just ignore him in certain cases.

So, whose fault is it? We could lift a strong finger and direct it towards your son's neurobiology, your parenting expertise, your family history, his trauma, bad luck, or anything else. But it doesn't matter because all of those things are symptoms of the problem. Forget blaming. Forget whose fault it is. Let's get results. Regardless of the symptoms, it's a problem that can be solved. In order to solve it, we must first understand the two most important people in your life. Those people are one, your child and two, the person who's taking on all the risk of making him better, yourself.

The Mind of Boys with Behavioral Struggles

The thoughts, emotions, and behaviors of the defiant boy are very special. It's powerful (as you may have experienced). You strong-willed boy is often disruptive, destructive, demanding, depleting, degenerating, and even demoralizing. However, these are the same children every parent loves the most, every teacher remembers, and everybody admires. Why is that? These boys possess a talent they have yet to learn how to control. It consumes them to a point where they lash out, say hurtful things, and harm others. Their talent is the ability to leave a mark, an impression and to strike the chords of people's emotional state. A power such as that must be guided with proper care and attention. The reason why you'll love helping your son gain control of his habits is because the greatest leaders in the world are naturally defiant.

The people who leave the most prominent, everlasting impressions are those who trigger emotions. Let me guess, your biggest fear is that your son will end up hurting you, themselves, or a loved one. Understandable. Or you believe he will end up in prison. You know who else's parents had that thought.... Richard Branson, a man with a net worth of 4 billion dollars and control of over 400 companies. The point is, your child has a powerful energy that is very negative, but after reading this book, learning from the experiences of others, and integrating best practices from industry leaders, you'll have the keys to turn that negative energy into a fruitful, positive energy used for good. Your child will go from unstoppable to unstoppable (don't let that go over your head).

Remember how we said, the same child who is disruptive and destructive is the same child every parent loves the most and who all the teachers will never forget? Well, that's because these kids force you to engage with them. You can't sit around and let them hit, kick, scream, interrupt, and be rude to people. They force you to invest. You're investing now. You're investing in reshaping their behavior. The more we invest in any person or item, the more attached we become. You could pay twenty dollars for a jacket and feel like you got the greatest deal in the world. When you take it home, you don't care if people touch it and throw it in a pile of clothes with everyone else. Conversely, you could pay two thousand dollars for the exact same jacket and completely lose it if someone even thought about touching that jacket without washing their hands first. Nothing changed besides your investment. You care more when you invest more. That struggle of the ups and downs, progressions and regressions, hardships and triumphs, are what make anything in life something meaningful. You're trying to solve the hardest puzzle of your life here. Ask a teacher which student they remember throughout the years, and it's the child that gave them stress. They never remember the kid who always listened and was quiet because he didn't force them to engage. It's why you love your son with all the struggles he may bring. You're invested in seeing him change, grow, and develop into someone better. Heck, you've probably seen glimpses of a beautiful soul and sit there and wonder, why can't he be like that all the time. Well, he can. But first, let's understand the four reasons why a boy says no, does not listen, and refuses to compromise.

1. He knows he can

Kids have an extremely high sense of social awareness. They are always looking for who is the leader and the follower in certain groups. In one moment, they process whether they will be able to get away with defiance by testing you. For example, when I began working with one child, he told me that he missed his old provider and that he did not like me. What did I say? I responded by saying, "oh, that's nice". What does "oh, that's nice" communicate? Well, I knew what he was doing. He was testing if I was going to fall into his frame of mind and react to his comment. If I reacted and said, "really, why, what did I do?", it would have given him all he needed to know that he can control me. He can press a button and I'll move like his puppet. Obviously, he is not smart enough to know this consciously, but he runs these tests on everyone he comes in contact with to determine how much he can trigger them. Responding with nonchalant lines like "oh that's nice" subconsciously communicates to him that I'm in my world, he's in his world, and we can share the world together. However, if he crosses a line, I leave him alone or dominate his world.

People often forget how closely related us magnificent humans are to the simplistic animals in the wild. In the wild, if an animal sees another, it's prepared to attack or run away, also known as the "flight or fight" response. The animal that stands their ground with confidence and conviction will usually dominate the other. We've all seen ferocious cats scare the living hell out of a human sized rottweiler. That dog can basically eat that cat for a meal but hey, that cat plays no games. It's determined and takes no crap from anyone. Humans are animals. We have those same instincts. We can sense the alpha males and females around us simply based off their body language. If you're worried that you don't have the tools to achieve such a demeanor, the answers will be clearly laid out for you later on.

Some parents say, "well my child does not respond well when I try to enforce rules or be dominant". The response is always, "It's not what you do that shows dominance, it's *how* you do it". People confuse dominance with being direct, rigid, strict, confrontational, and having a "my way or the highway mentality". They think you have to be serious, mean or disrespectful. In fact, I possess none of those qualities. I'm a fun guy who treats people well and actually hates confrontation. But if there's one thing I have, it's extreme personal boundaries. No matter how big or small you are, you can communicate with your son in a way that signals to him, "that kind of behavior will not be tolerated". It's a switch in your eyes, facial expression, and tone of voice. Establish boundaries with direct or indirect communication. More on the technical ways to achieve that later. Boys will show defiant behaviors because it is allowed by the teacher, parent, coach or guardian. Nearly all of these boys will act differently on a moment-to-moment basis depending on the adult that's leading them.

2. *They do not feel like you understand them*

This is "the world is against me" mentality. Most defiant boys have this. They think nothing is their fault and that everyone blames them for something they didn't do. In fact, you're probably laughing right now because they probably repeat those lines over and over again. "I didn't do it". "He did it first". "It's not my fault". I'll let you in on a little secret here. The best way to cure this mentality is to make sure your son has a good friend. Most defiant boys do not have a friend who they're emotionally attached and connected to. They may be social and outgoing, but still do not have that group they belong to, which is essential for feeling understood and like you can trust a fellow human. It's no wonder that no matter how much love you give to your son, he can always hate you because he still does not feel like you relate to him.

3. They like to do it for fun and enjoy attention

We all have it in us. Your son just likes to use it a little more. Seeing people react to what we do and say makes us feel good. It makes us feel like we're in control. Sometimes, it's just fun to mess with people's minds. You have to remember that you're dealing with a boy here. Little boys like to be reckless, wild and carefree in a physical way. It's a rush of adrenaline they get from that level of activity. One of the worst things you can do as a parent is to never let your son be a bit reckless. As long as he's not causing harm to himself or others, let him scream a bit or roll around on the floor. He needs to release that energy and if you try to control every little thing he does, it irritates him and further damages your relationship. Why is that? Remember reason number two - he feels like you don't understand him.

4. They like to do their own thing

Boys with oppositional defiant disorder and more diagnoses run to help their siblings, but then will hit their siblings when their siblings try to help them. It makes no sense until you understand that this kid just wants to do it *his* way. Helping you is doing what he wants, but your help for him actually interferes with him doing things his way. The best way around this issue of defiance is to offer choices, let him do things by himself with your supervision and letting him make his mistakes before you tell him what to do.

One, some, or all of those four reasons makeup why your son does not listen or defies you. The reasons can change in each situation. The fifth reason is their medical diagnoses if they have one. Any medical diagnosis where the child's neurobiology and chemical composition of their brain differs from the normal child is obviously a reason behind their actions. However, those diagnoses tell you more of what's going on, rather than how to deal with it. Right now, you're discovering how to identify and relate with your son regardless of his diagnosis so that you have empathy and understanding moving forward. After the next chapter, this book is all about actions to take that will help you deal with those behaviors every single time.

Chapter 2: Parenting Principles

No Excuses

One time a parent said, "he just can't help himself; his brain tells him to do it, you can't control him, it doesn't matter what I do, none of that stuff works on him". She was speaking to me in a way that was rather aggressive, but I understood where she was coming from. As a parent of a boy with behavioral struggles, you're often afraid of telling people that you struggle to manage your child. People respond by saying, "just punish him", "my child doesn't do that", "send him to a military school", "I can't picture him doing that" or "nothing is wrong, he's acting just fine right now". We only feel what we see. If we see someone with a nasty gash on their leg or a dislocated finger, we squirm in our chairs. Yet, we can't see the dysfunctions of a brain on the surface so it's hard to believe another person if we can't see their pain for ourselves. It's a huge problem for those who experience mental health issues. You can't put a band-aid on the brain. People say all of those naive statements because they're not thinking about you. They're imagining themselves in your shoes and simply guessing on what they would do. The don't have to dread the fact that putting a kid to bed can take an extra 30 minutes to an hour if he gets triggered at night. But I digress. Back to the mother I was speaking with.

After giving her a few tips, she considered me to be one of those outsiders who didn't understand. She thought I was telling her to use some of these tactics in this book and that all her problems would disappear. She thought it would be easy. No, it's never easy to change another human being, it's just possible. I told her she can be mad at me, herself or the world, but there is still no excuse. We are still left with a problem...your son's behavior. The reason excuses are non-existent around these parts is because saying there is nothing you can do leads to giving up. Yes, there may be something terribly wrong with your son, but I've worked with kids who had "terribly wrong" circumstances and watched them blossom into something amazingly right. There is no excuse because if you don't do anything, his chances of improvement diminish from 1 out of 100 to 0 out of 100. There is no excuse because someone who has had it worse has also prevailed. It's your job to be easy on yourself and patient with your boy, but also to never give up or give your son excuses for his behavior. Some moments, you will have to chalk it up to him having a disorder or bad day. That's fine. We're playing the long game here. You can modify his behavior. You can guide him. You can see him become his best self. The little moments where you show perseverance truly add up over the years if you stick with it.

What Makes You a Rare Parent?

The CDC reports that parent training in behavior management, child behavior therapy, and CBT works well for ADHD, disruptive behavior disorders, depression, anxiety, and PTSD. It should be the first step of treatment before medication. Here at Kidshapers, we believe you should try every natural remedy, tactic, and strategy before giving your child medicine with tons of side effects. I doubt you're lazy, otherwise you wouldn't be here today. On top of that, Medicaid costs for children using behavioral health services average at more than $8,000 per child, compared to physical health services around $2,000 per child. The worst case scenario from reading this book is that you learn one tiny little tactic or mindset shift to at least subside some of your son's behaviors. Even with that tiny information, you'll be saving yourself and others tons of money over the years. The third reason why you're so special and rare is because you'll help progress the criminal justice system. About 70% of incarcerated inmates show signs of mental health issues. If these issues were handled properly with care early on when they were children, these prisoners would be productive citizens gaining support for their illnesses rather than being punished for it. These inmates also may have had terrible trauma and parents who probably did not care as much as you. Seeing their moms, dads, and grandparents read about parenting and being better providers had the same chance of them being struck by lightning on a sunny day. However, you may be a friend of one of these parents who are struggling. They don't have to read this book, but if you learn anything from the material as we move forward, hold yourself responsible for sharing one small tip that you believe would help them tremendously. The last powerful purpose you serve is pushing our economy forward. If your son is filled with healthy emotions and mentalities, he will far outdo his competition in the workforce because he received treatment that made him self-aware of his strengths and weaknesses. He'll know the right path to take for himself.

So, after all is said and done, you'll join the family of revolutionary parents who saves money in healthcare, who improves our criminal justice systems, who supports parents in need and who invests in their own future. You are the rare parent and there's one final thing you should understand before we begin training; yourself and your parenting style. There are seven archetypes you'll fit into as a parent. Listen closely and see which one fits you best.

Parent Archetypes

"The Authoritarian Parent": This is the parent who tries to argue and overpower defiant children. They rely firmly on consequences and threats, but lack in listening and understanding their child.

Qualities

- Strong personal boundaries

- Speaks in a boss tone (downward vocal inflection)

- Gives direct commands

- Does not speak more than what's necessary

- Cares about protecting their ego and will try to win at all costs

- Loves to lecture

- "My way or the highway" mentality

- Enjoys control

"The Passive Parent": The parent who seeks permission from their son. They like to try to work with him and understand him but struggle terribly when he is out of control. Their son does not listen because the parent does not demand respect or command the room.

Qualities

- Weaker personal boundaries

- Repeats commands often

- Rarely yells

- Hates confrontation

- Feels sympathy for child

- Doesn't like to see him triggered or upset so tries avoiding it all costs

- Makes empty threats

- Very nice and people-pleasing

"The Scattered Parent": This is the parent whose life is a bit unorganized. They may be very creative, but lack structure and self-discipline which bleeds into their son's behavior as well. This parent is super supportive of their kids being themselves so it's hard for the parent to stop or control the child when it's necessary. These types of parents do not seek help often because they don't think anything is wrong.

Qualities

- Very anxious

- Easily triggered and reactive

- Poor listeners

- Lacks structure and discipline

- Often seems out of sorts

- Easily stressed

- Low self-awareness of habits

- Procrastination prone

"The Orderly Parent": This parent hates chaos. They enjoy thinking about the worst that can happen before thinking about the best that can happen.

Qualities

- Rule follower
- Cares deeply about a specific way tasks should be done rather than just getting it done
- Enjoys routine
- Hates chaos
- Hates wild behavior
- Self-conscious
- Worried about what other people think
- Safety-oriented
- Very professional
- Asks for advice or help before doing something on their own

"The Fun Parent"

Qualities

- Cool and nonchalant
- Places bond with kids as #1 priority
- Likes to joke around
- Tends to avoid making things serious or a big deal
- Low stress
- Usually positive and optimistic
- High energy

- Can lack structure, order, or discipline

- Lazy about things they do not agree with or understand

- Not easily embarrassed by child's behavior

"The Reserved Parent"

Qualities

- Introverted

- Does not do too much or too little

- Places self-care as #1 priority

- Follows their own rules

- Lacks the energy to manage child behaviors

- Extremely confused or unable to relate to child

- Likely to seek help from a professional

- Usually positive, but hard to motivate

- Likes clear-cut, simple communication

"The Empathetic Parent"

Qualities

- Approachable

- Caring

- Warm

- Great listener

- Will try to say yes at all costs

- Loves to help

- Cares about the team more than themselves

- Can sometimes be pushed around by more aggressive people

Parents who combine empathetic, authoritarian, and fun will have the most success managing boy behaviors. On the other hand, parents who are scattered, orderly, reserved, and passive will have the toughest time managing behaviors of defiance. The best parents know when and how to use qualities of all archetypes at the right moments. Now of course, no one is boxed into one archetype because no one acts the same way at all times. We bend and shape towards other tendencies depending on the circumstances. However, you probably fit into one archetype most of the time.

Now it's time to focus on your mindset as a great parent. Reshaping your psychology is just as important as reshaping your little guy's behaviors. Remember, it's not what you do, it's how you do it. Let's jump into some core principles, phrases and stories that will shape your mindset to be well-equipped to confidently and successfully handle behavioral problems in boys.

7 Core Principles That Make A Great Parent

In all the parenting forums, groups, Q&A's and meetings, there's one person who always asks the same question. It's the question you want to know. It's the question we all want to know. What makes a good parent? In truth, there is no right way to achieve the gold star of parenting. Actually, let me rephrase that. There's plenty of right ways to be an amazing parent. We all know that behaviors such as neglect and abuse are the worst ways to parent, but these core principles are what you need to know to reach the above average parent status. The average parent has no deliberate parenting strategy which means that their parenting efficiency is going to be highly influenced and comparable to the way they were raised by their parents; hints the good or bad parenting cycle. We'd also be ignoring reality if we didn't acknowledge that a person's parenting style could be heavily influenced by the partner they choose as well. Regardless, incorporating and adopting these principles will certainly shape every decision you make. You'll start to see your blind spots and your relationship with your son is about to get ten times easier. These are the 7 core principles that make a great parent, particularly for boys with behavioral needs.

Principle 1: Stern & Patient

When giving directions, give them with a stern tone of voice. Slightly raise your voice or add more power using your diaphragm, but there's no need to yell. Sternness mixed with patience is the ultimate formula. A person who speaks with conviction usually does not need to rush another person because their tone of voice already assumes the job will get done. Sternness mixed with impatience simply makes you a tyrant.

Principle 2: Your Child is Not Your Clone

Many parents struggle with this one, not just parents of boys with discipline issues. It's natural for a parent to try to make their children act, think, and be like them or someone that they admire. Heck, you're the one raising him, right? Yes, you are, but one day your child has to become their own person. Your job is to guide them into finding their strengths, not trying to make them into something you always imagined them becoming. That's extremely selfish on the parent's part and unfair to the child. If your child wants to be just like you and they decide to follow you, that's a different story. Here's the difference between the two. The wrong way... "You can't do that because that's not the way I raised you". The right way.... "I don't think you should do that, but if you really want to, you have to at least present your plan and then we'll agree on the best way you can accomplish it".

Principle 3: Say It Until It Gets Old

You should have common phrases you say to your child often when giving discipline and guidance. Here are some examples. Adopt them or use them as inspiration to make your own.

1. "You make things hard for me when I want you to do something, I make things hard for you when you want to have fun." This one is often used for cleaning up, homework or bedtime compliance.

2. "Everything is in your control; I respond based on your decisions." This is a great one to say in three types of situations: when you give a command, if your son is trying to make excuses for his behavior or when your son is freaking out from you giving consequences.

3. "What's making you feel that way?" (Instead of "why do you feel that way") Asking "what's making you feel that way" removes the insinuation of attack/judgement towards your child. We'll dive deeper on this phrase later on, but this phrase helps you give your son a voice and allow him a chance to explain his behavior. However, it does not mean that because he explains himself, he will get away with his behavior or won't be given consequences.

4. "Don't let the past be your future." This is a good reminder for your son that tells him to get his behavior back on track after he regresses.

There's plenty more to use as examples, but the point is to say the same thing over and over again, so it sticks in his brain. It makes things much easier for you as well because you don't have to think about what to say all the time.

Principle 4: Leadership Means Getting People in Sync

Growing up, I always defined leadership as being the person that others follow. However, I noticed the best leaders are those who take the little actions to make sure everyone is in sync. This is important for you to know because you and your son must live in harmony. You do this by communicating about every little thing, creating a culture of accountability and making sure expectations are clear. The best leaders do not get people to follow them, the best leaders are those who keep people synchronized.

Principle 5: Agree First

Agreeing with an opposing person first before giving your thoughts and feedback enables the other person to feel understood and cared for. If you don't agree first, they become defensive and try to argue. Agree first, and then make your point. For example, say "I could see why you were mad, that was a pretty mean thing for your friend to do, but if you hit him, you end up in a worse spot". That sounds much differently than, "you shouldn't have hit him because now you're in a worse spot".

Principle 6: Recognize and Appreciate

When your son comes home and takes out his homework immediately, you have to recognize and appreciate him for that. When he listens on the first command, you have to tell him "great job for listening the first time, that's a big boy move". When he respects his siblings and peers' personal space, you have to tell him "I like the way you acted there, that's what we always talk about, great job". Plain and simple, positive reinforcement builds confidence. When you recognize and appreciate behaviors, your son will want to be more consistent with his positive gestures as it automatically ties into our final principle.

Principle 7: Use Positive Labels

In order for you to understand the power of this last principle, I'd like to share some stories with you.

A parent once asked, "Victor, how important are the things we say to our kids on a daily basis"? Hmm how about very! In an absolutely dynamic scene from the television series, Power, a character named Dre, an ambitious drug dealer from New York, was inside his mother's home one night. His mother expressed why she does not trust him, why she thinks he is evil, and how upset she is about the fact that she can't see where she went wrong with raising him. He replied by giving her a vivid memory from when he was six years old. He said because he stole a silly little candy bar from one of his mother's friend's house, his mother began calling him a little demon and thief from that day forward. He was negatively labeled with words.

In his documentary on Netflix, Mike Tyson described his childhood. He initially got his respect from beating up a bully who was older than him after the boy snapped Mike's bird's neck. Everyone in the neighborhood began to like him and respect him because he stood up for himself. However, it quickly became a part of his identity to use physical domination to get his way. It wasn't until his first boxing trainer would tell him every day that he's the best, that he's unstoppable, and that he's ferocious, that Mike thought he could be great. If it weren't for his training feeding him bigger dreams and visions of a legendary career, Mike Tyson would likely have been dead or in prison. Luckily, he was positively labeled.

What results from labeling are adults like Dre, Mike or so many others who have unresolved trauma from their childhood. The words and actions we take as adults are crucial to our children's development. If you're a parent looking for a real New Year's resolution, try telling your son he is a good child who is loved dearly once a day for a whole year straight. Set a reminder on your phone or do whatever you must do. Words matter. The same way that telling a child they are bad can easily become a part of a so-called "bad child's" identity is the same way that telling them they're the best, they're loved, and that they are amazing can create positive identities. Positive labels create positive people.

Stay Disciplined

If you read the biographies of successful businessmen and businesswomen, you'll find that they had some defiant behavior when they were young or have strategic defiant behavior as adults. It makes total logical sense that someone who does not enjoy listening to others ends up building their own empire. That's what success takes. But as a parent, I'm sure you are more afraid of your child not going that route and you believe they will end up in prison. That's why we're going to teach you how to correctly guide the defiant behavior instead of trying to eradicate it. Your son will still remain fueled by that strong willpower, except the only difference is now you can rest at night knowing his power will be used for good.

Start by rethinking your commands and what behaviors are "wrong". For example, if your child is doing homework at the table, but they are standing up, most parents will bother their child to get them to sit down. But why do they have to sit down? They are still getting the work done right? You must choose your battles. If you get on your child about every small thing, it causes them to become anxious and annoyed. When dealing with a defiant child, give them space to be free as long as they are not harming other people, being destructive, or breaking laws (all of which lead to a prison cell). As the parent of a defiant child, you can't expect your child to follow the rules of everyone else. They are different. Take some time to yourself and figure out where you are being too overbearing with your child. Loosen up on some things and get more serious about others. You need to create your own playbook of rules and boundaries that are specifically tailored to your son.

Next up is developing a routine for your son. Ahh yes, as you can see, we're diving into the basics a bit late. How ironic. Are you making sure your boy is going to bed early enough with at least 8 hours of sleep each night? Is it the same time every night? Do they have the tv on when going to bed? Do they have designated homework time, creative time, and leisure time? What's the diet looking like? These are all supportive factors that make reshaping behaviors an easier or more difficult task. If you were not raised with a strict bedtime, then you may not appreciate how important it really is to your livelihood. There's a hundred pieces of evidence that explain the importance of sleep schedules, healthy eating, and being productive but let's keep it simple for you. The human brain always strives to minimize time and effort in everything we do. Imagine how stressful brushing your teeth would be if every night your toothbrush was in a different room, the toothpaste changes to a random flavor, and your tube was a different shape. However, the reason why brushing your teeth is easy and stress-free is because you put your toothbrush and toothpaste in the exact same spot every single day. You know what to expect. The same applies to your son and his behavior.

If you can set up a routine schedule for them, it makes their life less hectic, which then makes your life less hectic. Establishing a routine literally frees up space in our brains to focus on more important things. Your child will never see a bigger picture if all day they have to think about rudimentary habits such as bedtime. With more mental capacity, they will abide by your rules and trust your directions. In fact, one of the most disturbing findings is that students who sometimes come from urban environments and exhibit defiant behaviors are not bad kids. They're just hungry. They aren't getting enough sleep. I don't know about you but if those two life essentials are missing for just one day, I act out too. I just feel "off". So, imagine dealing with that on a day to day basis. Learning is the last thing on the mind. All their brain is trying to do is survive. It's painful. They feel misunderstood and malnourished. The only natural response is for them to try to get someone else to feel their pain. How is that accomplished? They disrupt others and hurt them as well. It's a vicious cycle. As a parent, please make sure you handle as many of these essentials as you possibly can. A good diet, routine, and expectations are the number one step before trying any other methods.

Your ability to guide a boy with behavioral problems is based on your mindset. It's based on your frame control. This is one of my favorite topics and this is honestly where you see the biggest difference between a parent who gets compliance and a parent who gets defiance from boys. It's never what you do, it's how you do it. Your frame of mind is the deciding factor of how you achieve results. You never have to hit or yell at your child with the proper frame control. There's true power needed to look someone in the eyes and to ignore them. There's true power in hearing people out, but never arguing because you meant what you said so there's no need to debate. There's power in responding to situations and controlling the outcome rather than reacting to situations and feeling defenseless to the outcome. These are all dependent upon your frame of mind and self-control or what we call "frame control".

Defiant boys love to push their parent's buttons simply because they know that they can. You can take that power away from them by refusing to argue, always remaining calm, and holding your composure when they decide to act out.

A common tactic used to show frame control is to call out behaviors. This particularly works well with attention seeking behaviors. A common issue with defiant children is that they always need to be the center of attention and will do whatever it takes to achieve it. If your child fits into this category, you can tell because they love to interject in every conversation and love to see people get emotional. That's why they're natural masters of social intelligence. If you are hugging someone and your child tries to break it up, do not just let it pass. Address it. Literally tell them, "I have enough attention for everyone including you. I love you and you do not always need to be the center of attention. When you do that, it makes me not want to give you attention because you are being rude and selfish to other people when you do not have to be. The best way to get my love and affection is to continue being a good child because I love rewarding good behavior".

In a similar scenario, I once dealt with a child who never listened on first command, but he always did it for more attention rather than outright defiance. For example, the teacher would tell the classroom to line up at the door. My child would sit there and wait until everyone lined up just so the teacher could tell him over and over again the same command. Teachers would get frustrated because they never had the time to step back and look at the situation differently. The plan of action was to re-direct the teacher to keep quiet and proceed with the class. There were two ways to get compliance in this situation: 1. Ignore the child and not address his behavior or 2. Tell the teacher, "no that's okay we'll just leave him behind because he obviously wants attention (saying it loud enough so he would hear me)". This "callout" caused my child to get up on his own and try to catch up with the class by saying "hey, wait for me". Every time he caught up, I would say to him, if you do not listen the first time, you will be left behind. Calling out the behavior dismantles them.

Frame control is very important for defiant children especially when their defiance is accompanied with attention-seeking behaviors. As seen in the example above, the two can sometimes be mistaken or interchangeable. One adult may report the child as defiant whereas another sees attention seeking behaviors that can be solved easier with planned ignoring rather than trying to enforce more discipline. Regardless, enforcing discipline or the ability to properly ignore your child's antics boils down to one thing if you are going to be effective. That one thing is how well you can control your own frame of mind.

When your son gets angry, it seems as if his brain has gone blank. In fact, most children claim to experience this loss of control and "blankness" when they are triggered. However, they can quickly calm down based on how *you* react. Your ability to remain calm and unphased by your son's actions is what makes him trust you. These are the subtle qualities of unwavering leadership. A true leader always remains calm and unphased in the heat of the moment. If little Michael is tearing down your curtains, snatching items, hitting you, screaming that he hates you and more, the most important aspect of the situation is your reaction. Even slight laughter can be effective in this situation as it shows that you don't take your child's acts seriously. Now, the thought of "what the heck, that's extremely rude and disrespectful to my son" probably just crossed your mind. However, it's time to step outside your comfort zone and get creative. Slight laughter shows you're maintaining a positive, unwavering attitude towards the situation. Yes, it's extremely saddening to watch your child lose control, but these are the moments this book was made for.

These principles and mindsets will help you stay in control when things get out of control. Feel free to reread and use them as a guide. Now that you understand what your son, yourself, and both your mindsets can achieve, how about we get to teaching you how to be the parent, the teacher, the professional who gives world-class behavior management and discipline to your kids.

Chapter 3: You've Tried Everything...Except This

Now we get down to the nitty gritty. This is for the no nonsense parents. The parents who want straight up answers to their biggest questions and concerns. The parents who want hardcore training on the best methods of interventions, communications, and results. The parents who hate that I'm still leading into this section and are itching to hear the magic bullet to solve all their child's behaviors. Are you ready to take action and test these skills with your son? The main caveat to remember throughout this section is even though we're going over alternative ways to discipline does not mean that the conventional methods should be abandoned. For instance, just because your son has ADHD does not mean you can't tell him to sit down. It simply means that if he does not comply, then you should consider what he is going through before you lose your patience. Let's dive into some stories, scenarios, step-by-step solutions, and master techniques to equip you with the armor you need in the battle of guiding your boy to his best behavior.

The Intervention Formula

Based on experience and research, we developed a 10-step easy guide for parents to remember when performing interventions. If your son needs multiple interventions on a daily basis, then he'll likely need 1 on 1 services from a professional. Each step tells you what to do. If a child complies in phase I, then phase II steps are not always necessary. Visit www.kidshapers.biz to speak with myself or a team member to request deeper insight on this formula.

Phase I - Under Control

Step 1: Command - attempt your command in a calm, stern voice.

Step 2: Warn - tell the boy his consequence if he does not comply.

Step 3: Follow Through - tell him what privilege has been lost and follow through with taking it away. If you will take his privileges away at a later time, that's fine. Stay positive and move on past this situation for now until it's time for you to deliver later. Then skip to step 8.

Phase II - Out of Control

Step 4: Back Off - ignore or wait patiently, do not pressure your son as it will aggravate him further. Some of you have boys who have delays. A delay occurs when a child is becoming aware of what are compliant and noncompliant behaviors. He wants to be good, but sometimes his brain still tells him to be defiant. He will sometimes delay after a command in order to take an extra second to decide on whether he will comply or defy. If you pressure him, he will surely defy. Give him time to work through that delay by telling him the choice is his and you hope he makes the right one. This gives him power. Once he has power to decide, the only person he can oppose is himself. If you pressure him, it's you against him.

Step 5: Breathe - tell him to take 3-5 deep breaths and do it with him. I cannot stress this enough. Breathing is paramount because it's the one thing we can always control. In fact, in every single child I work with, breathing is the first thing I teach them to do. Breathing should be incorporated as a habit to return to a state of control when your son is excited, sad, angry, anxious, and frustrated. Meditation classes have been implemented in prisons and schools and have only produced positive results. It's time for the world to recognize and respect such a simple and powerful habit that we all should practice. C'mon, when's the last time you heard meditation *negatively* impact someone's life?

Step 6: Empathize - agree with him, see his side of the story and express concern.

Step 7: Follow Through - give the consequence and explain the positive outcome he receives from complying. For example, "because you decided to take your consequence like a big boy, I will cut it from 10 minutes to a 5 minute timeout, great job" or "the sooner you do what I asked, the sooner you can get back to playing".

Phase III - Shaping

Step 8: Verbalize - encourage him to verbalize what he felt and admit what he did wrong.

Step 9: Reenact - encourage him to re-do his actions after he understands the correct way to do it. Very simple philosophy here. Practice things the right way and that's how you perfect it.

Step 10: Congratulate - positively reinforce any positive takeaways your child accomplished and give a high five or other gesture. This is the glue to your poster. If you miss this step of positive reinforcement, all your hard work falls off the poster onto the floor and you must start over.

Let's recap.

Step 1: Command

Step 2: Warn

Step 3: Follow Through

If he becomes triggered (which means he is losing control) continue with step 4. If he is not triggered, skip to step 8.

Step 4: Back off

Step 5: Breathe

Step 6: Empathize

Step 7: Follow Through

Step 8: Verbalize

Step 9: Re-Enact

Step 10: Congratulate

During timeouts, always take the time to explain what your son did wrong. Question them on what they should have done instead by saying, "how do you think you could have handled that differently" or "Do you think if you tried ... (insert a more acceptable solution) that you would be standing here in trouble right now". There is nothing bad about telling a child when they are wrong. Being told they are wrong in a respectable manner is something kids need to get used to for the real world. If they never understand that making mistakes and being wrong are okay, then they'll get defensive and ego-stricken anytime someone criticizes them. Their game will be thrown off by the smallest amounts of judgement because they were never taught how to perceive and overcome their shortcomings in a healthy manner. After respectfully and empathetically telling them what they did wrong, follow that up by giving them the correct solution and it provides a huge amount of value. There's nothing wrong with him (or you) making mistakes as long as you're taking deliberate action and focus to be better in the future. However, if telling your child that they are wrong triggers them into an argument or more anger, baby step your way into this principle.

Usually when you ask questions such as what could you have done differently to avoid getting in trouble, he will say "I don't know". This is where you break down the scenario and/or role play with him to provide a concrete impression of the more acceptable behavior. Let's say Robert hits his sibling whose name is Nicky. You give Robert a timeout and he is angry. During the timeout, you ask why he hit Nicky. He says because Nicky hit him first (the most common response every child gives). The common response most parents use is "well why didn't you tell me first before hitting him back" or "you should have told me before you decided to hit him back". However, I challenge you to ask the same question just in a different way. Ask him, "what should you have done"? He'll likely respond, "I should have told you". Usually when a child responds like this, their tone of voice shifts into one of sorrow and guilt. They think, "yeah, I know that's what I should have done". It automatically makes them partially accountable whereas telling them what to does not have much of the same effect. When kids verbalize what their actions should have been, it makes them take ownership rather than just listening to another person tell them what to do (which could trigger their oppositionality). It's the difference between listening to a speech and giving a speech. Two completely different ideas, right? When they hear, "why didn't you tell me" or "you should have done", they perceive it as an attack.

Another way to shift perspective is to show your son what well-behaved kids do in similar situations. This shadow method is where the child is on the outside looking in. They are seeing things from your vantage point. Usually a well-behaved child tells the adult first because that's what they were taught to do, and they follow directions pretty well. Show that to your son if the opportunity is available, but of course avoid telling him to be like another child. No child or person likes to be told that they should act like someone else. Simply say, "I am not trying to say you have to act exactly as this child, but they are following directions, so they always get to have fun. I just want the same for you, so that's why I wanted you to watch them".

Master Techniques

In this section you'll get an exclusive sneak peek into some of the master techniques that will be used in our upcoming eProgram. Most of the techniques involve special training where plenty of context is needed in order for them to be clearly understood and executed. You can stay up to date on when the program is available by visiting www.kidshapers.biz

Asking Questions

This strategy will be further discussed in the next chapter. Instead of telling the child what to do, ask what they should have done. This works well if you have already explained and established solutions to a problem beforehand. It's similar to tutoring. Holding a position as a peer tutor in college algebra and trigonometry, my method was to show fellow students how to do the problem first. However, after they told me they understood how to solve it, I would make them guide me through the problems simply by asking them leading questions rather than continuing to give them the answers. Work through and agree on acceptable behaviors with your son. Once the answers are established, you practice. When your son gives you the answers to the questions of his behavior, he retains the information better. Teach it, make sure he understands, and from then on, ask questions.

Explain Yourself

Tell your son what you are doing and why you do it to teach him a valuable lesson. Kids are very curious and uninformed about the way the world works so it's your job to teach them. Always explain why you do everything. He should know why he has to get up early for school, why he has timeouts, why he loses privileges, why he earned your praise, why you love him, why he should not hit, why he should be respectful and everything else in the world. Without you explaining, he just takes your words and actions as attacks to destroy his freedom. The only time you do not explain yourself is in the midst of an argument or when you know one is about to begin. In these cases, explaining yourself enables the argument.

Verbalize

Adopt the habit of encouraging your son to verbalize or repeat what you said to them, what they are about to do, or what they should do. For example, you tell your son that he can go back to playing once he apologizes to Joel for hitting him. In this case, he needs to verbalize it three times. After you explain what he is going to do and why he is going to do it, he is going to say to you, "I am going to say sorry for hitting my friend, Joel. I am going to tell him that it won't happen again. Then I can go back to playing after apologizing." You will say, "good job, that's right, now show me I can trust you and that you're a big boy by telling Joel the same thing. I want to hear it loud and clear or you have to do it again". Then he will go to Joel and say, "Joel, I was angry and I'm sorry for hitting you, it won't happen again". Then you will say, "nice job buddy. What did you learn or what did you do that was so great there?". He will verbalize it for the third time, or you can verbalize it for him to show positive reinforcement and approval. When kids verbalize and speak the words out loud, it forces them to take ownership and pride. In reality, he may hit Joel again five minutes later, but the point is, over time if he keeps telling himself he won't do it because it's wrong, his conscious mind will catch up and he will break the habit of hitting when he is angry.

"End-Sents"

No, not incense like the sticks you burn for a delightful smell. "End-Sents", short for end of sentences, is a Kidshapers term for questions meant to be said at the end of sentences to check in and establish a collaborative frame. For example, "Do you agree", "what's your thoughts on that", "do you understand why", etc. It's a natural form of communication for some parents. However, some parents do not use it and that's an issue. As you may have noticed, these "end-sents" are used as an entry tactic into you using the master technique of explaining yourself. It allows you to gauge how much your child is comprehending your lessons and understanding his behaviors.

This next one is a bit long, but I'll start off asking you a question that I should have asked a long time ago. Are you a single mother? A single father? Are you a co-parent? Are you a solo teacher or do you have an assistant? This next strategy is commonly known across the world. You've seen it played out in all the comedies and all the action-packed crime shows. The good cop, bad cop strategy works extremely well for co-parents. This method can be difficult for single parents due to its polarizing, opposite nature, but let's dive into some ways both sets of parents can use this tactic to get compliance.

Good Cop, Bad Cop

Edward absolutely hates when playtime is over, but today is a day where you cannot tolerate any kind of overtime. The family must catch a flight in a few hours to go visit relatives for the Christmas holiday. If you miss your flight, you'll be stuck at the airport due to the snowstorm headed in town. You politely ask Edward to turn the television off and to clean up. At first, he says okay and you breathe a sigh of relief only to come back 10 minutes later to find him glued to screen not having moved one muscle. You try to stay calm but the sense of urgency builds. You tell him again to turn the tv off and explain that you need him to cooperate so he can go visit grandma. You tell him all about the presents he's going to get and the good food waiting for him. He smiles about it and says he's not done watching his show. You can't sit there and talk. What do you do? The nice and calm training tactics just are not working. Next thing you know, your husband comes storming in with high energy, urgently turns the tv off and says, "let's go everyone!" Edward gets moving and packed. You're just sitting there like, "wow, if I would've done that, Edward would have snapped". You're probably right. See this scenario is very uncommon and you're about to hear how it usually goes down. But let's focus on why this one *would* work first. You basically seasoned and prepped the chicken and your husband put it in the oven. Edward was so caught up in your patience and agreeable approach that he almost didn't even notice dad's aggressive, demanding style. Remember, defiant children are defiant because they feel attacked. The reason why Edward wasn't triggered in this situation is because he didn't feel alone. Dad's aggression seems geared towards everyone, including you. It's the difference between a teacher saying, "the whole class is missing recess today" compared to "Edward is missing recess today". It removes the personal attack.

Alright, let's switch this around to how things usually go down. Edward is watching TV in his room; dad comes storming in demanding that the family is in a rush to catch their flight and Edward needs to get dressed right away. Edward complains that he does not want to leave, he screams no and argues until hairs turn gray. Dad turns off the tv, leaves the room saying to Edward, "you heard what I said, I won't repeat myself". Now Edward shuts down, refuses to get dressed and makes multiple attempts to turn the TV back on. He definitely feels attacked. He doesn't care if dad is giving everyone the same attitude, Edward only cares about himself. Edward is enraged and won't speak a word even when he's been threatened to get all his privileges taken away. The goal here is to get the family on the flight. As the good cop, you can either walk in there and tell him, "what did your father say" (which will get you 0% progress towards that goal) or you can take these next steps which will work like a charm.

Step 1: Approach your child with a smile and a handshake or a high five.

Step 2: Address his desires.

Step 3: Ensure that you'll make sure your child gets what he wants, just at a later time.

Okay, let's see the inner workings of these simple steps in more detail.

Step 1: Let dad leave the room and approach your child with a smile and a handshake or a high five. This step is vital. The smile is important because you're positive. It seems like you're oblivious to what just happened. What does this do? This opens Edward up immediately because he feels like you aren't on Dad's side and he thinks he'll be able to get you on his side by telling *his* side of the story. The handshake or hi five is crucial because it's rather difficult to reject someone's hi five or handshake. Think about it. Anytime someone gives you a smile and a hi five with great energy, how does that make you feel? You feel automatically closer to that person and open to their approach...even if they're a stranger or even if you're in a terrible mood. Once again, it has the same effect of opening your child up for communication. You don't have to say a word. Just smile and hi five.

Step 2: Address your child's desires. This is simple. Keep the positive, light, nonchalant energy and simple say, "oh were you watching Marty's Playhouse, that's a good show". Edward will probably say, "and yeah dad made me turn it off" or he'll remain quiet in shutdown mode.

Step 3: Ensure that you'll make sure your child gets what he wants, just at a later time. You finish this good cop, bad cop scenario by saying, "yeah Dad can be a bit harsh from time to time, but we're in a really big rush to go see your grandparents. You know what that means right? It means I get to tell grandma how much of a good boy you've been, and you know she'll give you extra cookies for that. On top of that, if we miss our flight, you'll miss your presents and we don't want that do we" (Side Note: use the term "we" instead of "you". Remember, teamwork can remove the feeling of loneliness and attack with defiant children). Edward replies, "no, I don't want to miss out on my presents". You continue by saying, "yeah, I don't want that for you either so show me you're a big boy, let's get dressed and mommy will make sure you get to watch your show later, I promise". In this step, you're labeling Edward as a big boy and encouraging him to verbalize the fact that he does not want a particular consequence which is to miss his presents. Once the child verbalizes what they want, it's extremely rare that they'll continue to argue or defend their previous position because now they've committed to the new action. A golden strategy to always remember is to get your child to verbalize their actions. A child does not agree until they can verbalize.

Good cop, bad cop works well if you communicate with your partner. That way, if your child tries to put the parent's words against each other, you two discussed beforehand this would be a possible method of intervention. This helps to avoid arguments and ego-battles between you and your partner. The good cop, bad cop strategy is meant to do one thing and one thing only, get the child to comply with the initial command. It does not matter how it gets done, just as long as it does get done. Communicate this with your partner so the two of you avoid feeling any kind of betrayal or miscommunication towards the initiator's first approach. Remember at the beginning of this book for parent archetypes, we said that the best parents know how to switch and bend using various qualities from all the archetypes when the situation called for it. Well, this is exactly what we were insinuating here with this strategy. In every situation, for every child, I play the part of balance. Balance is the core value of the good cop, bad cop strategy. If a child has a parent or teacher who lets him run wild, I tend to play the disciplinarian. If a child deals with an aggressive, authoritarian adult, I play the role of the compassionate, empathetic, fun adult who is trying to give this child a voice so that he may feel heard and understood. Offering your child balance and breadth of experiences is a key principle of a great parent. That's how they create well-rounded, successful young adults.

So, to recap;

Step 1: Approach your child with a smile and a handshake or a hi five.

Step 2: Address your child's desires.

Step 3: Ensure that you'll make sure your child gets what he wants, just at a later time.

As a single parent, this strategy is difficult due to the fact that it involves taking on a polarizing identity. You can't switch from good cop to bad cop all at once because it resembles a lack of self-control on your part. Your child would think that you are indecisive in your leadership which could negatively impact their behaviors and possibly cause them to reenact those same mannerisms through the effects of modeling. In other words, they'll start to behave with sporadic behaviors going from bad to good (and good to bad) in rapid fashion because that's what they see you doing. In order to use this tactic as a single parent, it's highly advised that you give at least 30 minutes without interacting before switching to the other character.

Where Should You Go for Extra Help

You can go see a long list of child psychiatrists, counselors, psychologists, therapists, and social workers. Another option is the long, dark, lonely, tedious path of researching on the internet and getting back nothing but generalized information. There's plenty of places you could go, but none of them truly fit who you are and what your son is experiencing. On the other hand, Kidshapers offers an online group for you to share your story as you experience it on a daily basis. AA meetings use the same structure and approach because they know that when you give people a chance to share their story with those who are going through the same struggles, it offers peace, tailored advice, and ultimate support. It's important for you to have a voice and a community that supports you through a difficult patch in your life. What makes us a bit different from other groups is that if you signal that you need help with your boy's behavior, we comment with some quick tips or referrals to get you specialized support for your son. In addition, another mission of Kidshapers is to be the connector that brings together parents, school leaders, and teachers who share in our mission of improving child behaviors. We're building this group to be simple, results-oriented and specifically tailored to support people just like you who want to learn about child behavior. Even though our company is on the path of never-before-seen growth, we're still humble enough to understand that our information will not connect with every single family who deals with boys with behavioral issues. However, that's no excuse for our ability to serve. In saying that, we are in the process of building a directory of the best professionals, nonprofits and healthcare providers to serve parents just like you. That way, even if we can't help, we know someone who can fit your specific situation.

Parents, teachers and school leaders can visit www.facebook.com/weshapekids now to join our online group if this is something that sounds like a good fit for where you are. There is absolutely no better way to cope than to release your frustration with those who can relate to your story.

Private practice professionals, nonprofit organizations, and healthcare providers may contact us at www.kidshapers.biz for a potential partnership.

Chapter 4: The Day You Never Saw Coming

Now it's time to make you the master of understanding and shaping boy behavior. In the remaining chapters, all the beans will be spilled. It's time for the final secrets to be shared.

Asking Questions Part II

Asking questions helps you understand your child from their point of view. If you direct, request, and command all day long, your child will feel exhausted and even neglected. Compare your relationship with him to the one you have with your boss or superior. Your boss knows they have power and leverage over you, but would it be necessary for them to always make that obvious? In other words, when someone who has leverage over us takes the time to treat us with respect and genuine care, when they take an interest in us for who we are, not just what we can do for them, it means something very special to us. Your child feels the same way. Asking questions allows their feelings and thoughts to be heard. You don't have to agree with your child's answers or responses, but you should always be open to hearing them for the sake of their emotional health.

In general, you want to avoid 'why' questions such as "why did you do that", "why are you acting like this", "why can't you be this way", and so on. However, 'why' questions may be used *after* a 'who, what, when, or where' question. Examples of these types of questions are "what made you feel like you wanted to hit your brother", "where did you learn how to express yourself in that way", "when do you feel like you are losing control", or "who makes you feel bad". Ask these questions in an inquisitive, curious, compassionate tone of voice. Avoid using interrogation, irritated, or threatening tones. After your child answers one of these questions, then you may ask "why", in a caring tone of voice. For example, during a timeout, you ask your son "what made you want to hit your friend"? He responds, "he had the toy I wanted and didn't give it to me". You respond, "so how did that make you feel"? He replies, "angry!". Now you may ask the 'why' question by saying, "okay, so why do you think that makes you feel angry". He'll likely respond saying "I don't know or because I want it", something vague. Your next step is to make an agreement with him on how he should handle a similar situation moving forward. You express that you are not mad at him and you do not think he is bad, but you're worried that he will not have any friends if he continues to hurt them.

Take note here, the only command you've given is a timeout so far. Everything else has been questions meant to address your child's emotions, understand their triggers, and gain valuable information for future incidents. Regardless of how this conversation ends, you now already know from one intervention, one important thing that triggers your son, how he responds to these triggers, and what the two of you agreed he will do if he feels this way again. These are the nuts and bolts, the meat and cheese, the bread and butter of proper interventions. Asking questions leads to pertinent information compared to only giving timeouts or giving long lectures of why your child shouldn't behave a certain way. Ask questions, ask questions, ask questions!

How to Create Agreements with Boys

Once you establish agreements and contingency plans with your child, that's when your relationship becomes synchronized and much easier. Before we discuss the why and how, let's first understand what is this agreement? An agreement is the laws and step-by-step actions you and your child agree will be taken if a particular situation happens. These are usually derived from previous interventions such as the one stated in the previous example of your son getting angry and hitting their friend because the friend had a toy your son desired and wouldn't cough it up. An agreement is what you and your son declare are the appropriate steps to take when he feels angry, depressed, anxious, excited, impulsive, out of control, aggressive, or any other feeling that needs some fine tuning. Agreements make relationships much easier because you've been there before. You've been in this same emotional situation, but you've logically discussed how it should be addressed in the future.

We've said it multiple times, but let's say it again. When your son verbalizes what they will do in the future, they take ownership and it attaches to their pride and ego. It's similar to the effect of affirmations or the law of attraction. What they say is what they will eventually believe. What they believe is eventually how they will behave. How they behave determines their actions, outcomes, and results. So, when you and your child both verbalize and agree on steps to take in a particular situation, you feel much more confident and prepared to follow what you set forth. It makes things much easier on you because you won't have to spend time crafting a new intervention every time your son gets angry. You won't feel stressed and burnout from having to give an extremely long lecture. You don't have to yell. All you need to say is, what did we discuss and agree are the correct ways to handle our anger, to do when we feel down, and everything else your child experiences.

Agreements benefit your child to exceptional levels as it gives them a game plan, a safe haven to fall back on when you aren't around. When they're at school, on the field, or with friends, they are equipped to manage themselves. As you can see, in order for the agreement to be memorized, it must be repeated in the same steps. These steps should be optimized and restructured over time as the first agreement you craft together may just be a rough draft. We all must start somewhere, even this book. This book started off getting criticized and shredded by reviews, but we knew it wouldn't be perfect at first, it was a rough draft. We took no offense, made it better, and now it's creating the most harmonious adult-child relationships across the world. Your agreements are no different. You must start somewhere.

Begin by writing down your agreement with your son. Do not make it long. In fact, try to keep it as short and clear cut as possible. You're going to create different agreements for different feelings because they will require different interventions. The point is, you want to keep these short and sweet because things that are short, sweet, and meaningful are extremely easier to remember for our brains (hints the reason why motivational quotes work so well). Over time, you will refer back to this agreement until you and your child have it memorized. So, now we're at the 'how'. How do you create agreements? Some of you are sitting there impatiently saying, "c'mon victor, give me some examples man, I'm ready, stop playing". Well I have a question for you. Are you ready? No, no, are you *really* ready? See that. I'm teaching you a lesson inside a lesson. Your ability to joke around is paramount to the relationship and discipline with your child. You want compliance? You have to speak their language. A child's number one rule is to have fun and we'll discuss some more ways you can bond with your child later. Joking around, even in serious situations, keeps everyone feeling light, easy, and open for compliance. But alright, back to work, let's get to the example.

This book covers a lot of information on kids who are easily triggered and how to manage them when they are out of control. But on the other hand, some of you just have a kid who seems like he enjoys being a bad boy. He likes being rude, mean, and hurtful towards others. He may not even get triggered as much, but he just needs to learn how to treat people better. He's always fighting, making someone cry, or getting in trouble. He may even be a bully, but most parents do not see it as such. It's funny how every parent complains about bullies, but no one ever claims to be the parent of child who does the bullying. That's due to the reason that parents of bullies see their children as someone who needs help, or the parent is a bully themselves. In the first case, let's learn how to make an agreement with a child who is lost in the world of bad behavior. *He* is not bad. He just needs help being pulled out of the quicksand before it's too late.

First, it's important to note that these types of boys are little alphas. They're leaders. If you try to go against him, he'll rebel even harder. With these types of boys, talk to them like they are adults. Your tone and demeanor switch depending on how you perceive your son. Some kids you should talk to in a kid-friendly tone that's light, fun, and compassionate. But with most boys who have behavior problems, that usually goes out of the window. Phrases that work well with these little alphas are, "you like to have fun don't you", "you're a pretty tough guy", or "most kids don't understand, but you do". Lines like that instantly build rapport and he'll feel like you understand him on a level that no one else does. Once again, when you have rapport and a child respects you because you've shown that you can relate, compliance is 100 times easier. Your tone of voice is incredibly important when communicating with a boy on this level. Let's say his name is Christian. Talk to Christian as if you're on a team together and you're working towards a goal. The goal here is to get him to stop talking to people in an aggressive manner, to stop him from being so defensive and argumentative, and to stop him from antagonizing people to the point where it leads to physical altercations.

The agreement you establish is every time Chris argues, insults, or fights with someone, he has to compliment two others within the next hour. If he does not compliment two other people within that hour, he does chores around the house for the rest of the day. As you can see, we've already covered his positive treatment by giving him the option to compliment. He's focused on doing something positive for others or he has the decision to inflict a punishment on himself by losing his privileges for the rest of the day. Using punishments that focus on positives will make Christian's mindset and behaviors drastically improve. Now you're probably saying, "it's not that easy" or "my son is not going for that". If you are saying that, the rest of this book is going to cover how to make it easy. Everything is easy with your child if you can get compliance. So, if your child is not listening or does not agree to this after you explain it, he is not compliant. This form of agreement works well for those kids who are compliant but need positive ways to reshape their behaviors. It was designed for those parents that can recognize issues in their son and can get them to listen, but simply don't know how to replace their negative behaviors with positive ones. The next sections are for those parents who need some final ways to get their sons to listen, follow directions and become compliant.

Good Job. You Did It. Now Do It Right.

The definition of leverage is the power to influence a person or situation to achieve a particular outcome. That definition is perfect because it encapsulates the purpose of this book - influencing a person (boys with behavioral problems) and it describes our goal here - to achieve a particular outcome (amazing, positive behaviors). Without this method, there is no way you can begin to reshape behaviors for compliance. Without leverage, you are completely lost. It's absolutely ridiculous how stupid a child will make you look if you do not know what influences them to make decisions. The scariest part is that it's very common among parents to *not* use their leverage. That's why they become stressed out and start to lose faith in their parenting abilities.

Would you like to know what a parent without leverage looks like? Imagine watching 7-year-old Ryan, your best friend's son, taking a hammer and banging it into your friend's wall while you're at their house for a visit. Got the image? Good! Next, imagine your friend completely in shock, but for the sake of this example, there is no way she can snatch the hammer away or physically stop Ryan from continuing his good ol' "fun". What does she do as a parent who does not have leverage? This. She yells, "Ryan stop!", "You're going to have a timeout", "I'm going to spank you", "You're making me very angry", "5, 4, 3, 2...", "Why are you doing that", and more. What's the problem here? Nothing your friend is saying is actually a threat or warning to take away something *Ryan* wants. He does not care about a timeout. Time is not a scarce idea in a child's mind. They think it lasts forever. He does not care about a spanking. The pain will go away after a few minutes (Side note: if the pain does not go away after a few minutes, it's abuse. If you're giving spankings multiple times a month, it's abuse. Seek help from professionals who can correct your son's behavior or your perspective on his behavior.) He does not care about making people angry. He enjoys seeing them get worked up because it feeds him more attention and power to control their emotions. But Ryan does care about his iPad. He does care about watching tv. He does care about playing sports. He does care about playing with friends. He does care about dessert after dinner. This is leverage and this is what your friend should have used when trying to get Ryan to stop. Leverage is what Ryan finds most valuable.

Take some time to enjoy talking with your son. You will want to build a closer connection and learn about their favorite activities. That information will be used for bonding as well as your leverage which both combine into your vault of power for compliance. If your son's favorite toy is the fire truck, you're going to use this fire truck as leverage when giving warnings and following through with consequences (which will be discussed later). Now for those of you who do use leverage, you're probably irritated because you know it's never that easy. Sometimes your verbal warnings do not work, and your child continues with the defiance. You feel as if there is nothing else you can do in that situation and guess what, you're 100% correct. But wait, notice how I said, in *that* situation. Because his emotions and behaviors are brewing for an explosion, if you continue to pressure him, he'll burst. It's important to take the next steps which are to back off and follow through with consequences once Ryan calms down. This is the point where most parents fail at reshaping behaviors. They forget or lack the backbone to follow through.

We all want something in life and when it is taken away from us, we desire ways to get it back. Leverage helps you get compliance because it forces your child to make a decision. They either lash out or fall in line with your commands. Leverage is not always going to work. Sometimes your child just wants to act up and then you move on to the next phase of discipline. However, leverage will dramatically increase the percentage of your son listening on first attempt. Without leverage, you will be lost when making attempts to get compliance because your child isn't scared of losing anything. Your leverage could be sports, playtime with friends, video games, art time, or even eating time (**YOU MUST FEED YOUR CHILD or you will end up prison** - however making them wait 5-10 minutes before they eat with everyone else so that you may talk to them about their behavior is a last resort of leverage you could use). When you withhold something a child really wants, you have their full attention. That's when they will listen. A quick fix adults can make is to add an "or" statement after their requests. For example, "you should clean up or you won't be able to watch tv" and "You need to do your work or else you can't play". Most parents leave it at, "clean up please" or "do your work". They're giving commands, but they're setting themselves up to repeat it a thousand times over because they're missing leverage.

You are the parent...you control your child's life...not the other way around. You purchased the toys that they are using. You can lock those toys away. You give him attention. You can take it away. You allow him to have privileges. You can give consequences. Your son can be influenced to make the best decision for himself when his privileges are at stake. Figure out what your child enjoys the most, make a list, and practice taking each one away to see which one has the most impact on his discipline. Remember, use discipline that positively influences compliant behaviors for the long term. Be extremely careful about how your child responds. The last thing you want is for your son to repress his emotions and resent you. If your child becomes fearful, anxious, or shy around you, then you are headed down the wrong path. The kids I have worked with have always clearly understood when it was time to play and have fun around me and when I was serious. That line is drawn and displayed through the use of simple body language and vocal tonality which is coming up now.

Chapter 5: Keeping It Simple, Keeping It Powerful

If you have received any helpful information from this book so far, we'd love to hear it. Before you finish the book, share your insights with your fellow parent community by clicking <u>HERE</u> (https://www.amazon.com/dp/B084VTDC2L) to leave your review. Your voice is especially important to furthering the awareness of child behavior and mental health across the world.

Words Actually Do Matter

At an event supporting a non-profit for kids, families were allowed to take pictures of their kids receiving awards. I was able to see all types of people walk over to take their picture. Everything was going great until the pictures began for one family in particular. A little girl was in a group with other children her age. She was told by her aunt, the person taking the picture, to not smile because her smile was ruining the photo. The little girl was about 10 years old and she had a slightly awkward smile. As a matter of fact, it wasn't even awkward, it just was that forced smile that kids do from time to time. You know, how kids move their cheeks to smile but their eyes aren't smiling so it looks fake. Anyway, the little girl literally started shedding tears as her picture was being taken. Worst of all, the aunt made her try again and again while still shaming the girl. This was a small moment in the aunt's eye. It will pass. But I can assure you, this small moment creates a big change in this little girl's self-esteem for a lifetime. In fact, the aunt might deny she ever did that. She'll take pride in all the gifts she got for her niece during the holidays, all the trips she took for her, and all the times she cared for her niece when she was sick. In the aunt's mind, she's a loving, considerate, and sacrificing family member who loves her niece dearly. So, why did she have such a terrible moment?

Well, it's for the reason most parents inflict unintended harm on their child. It's because they are self-conscious and worried about what other people are going to say about their kids. The aunt is thinking about her desire to post the picture online and in her mind, everyone is going to laugh and judge her niece for smiling weird. So, she lets loose and violates her relationship with the person who really matters at the end of the day. As you may have realized, it's the little things that matter here. Your child may have never told you some of the things they remember you said to them that left them feeling vulnerable and unloved. When people hear trauma, they think of the worst forms of trauma. They think of parents throwing hot coffee at their kids, alcoholic uncles committing vile acts, and more. Yet, trauma is not based on the perpetrator, it's based on the victim and how they receive it which means that the slightest words can be traumatic. Being left alone in the house for 5 minutes can make a child lose trust in people forever. In those five minutes, the child can tell themselves they are left alone to fend for themselves and that concept could stick and alter relationships for the rest of their lives. Worst of all, it can become buried and unravel in other forms.

All of this is not intended to make you sensitive to everything you say or do because no one is perfect. It's simply giving you and others some context to be aware and to be empathetic towards your children. The gifts your children beg you for are totally irrelevant although on the surface it seems to mean the world to them. A parent once asked me, "how do I let my child know I love them without giving them everything they ask for"? I told him, "I'll put it to you this way. A child plays with toys for a day or two. They beg for it. They love it. They forget it when the next one comes along. But there's one thing that your child does not beg you for and it's the one thing that they never forget. That thing is how you make them feel. It's the way you treat, love, or care for them. The way you make a person feel is far more powerful than any tangible item you can find on a shelf". He shook his head to show that he understood. Do you?

Mastering Body Language

We consider body language a simple change many parents can make to get compliance. This is basic human nature and social skills that you never learn in formal education. This pillar is vital because body language is subtle, yet powerful. It's the tool that makes parenting completely effortless. If you want your presence to have purpose and meaning, you want to correct your eye contact when speaking to children, particularly boys with behavioral problems. In order to effectively lead, it's imperative to understand the appropriateness of using the correct tone of voice as well. Children are naturals at social communication and their emotional intelligence is off the charts. Their instincts are better than adults because they do not think as much as we do. They feel. So, as we dive deeper into subtle skills such as vocal tonality and eye contact, remember, do not force it. Body language is a blind spot that most people, including myself will not be able to properly assess unless someone else notices our tendencies or we record ourselves. No one wants to admit that they do not speak confidently to children and some do not even realize that they don't. Recording yourself and receiving personalized consultations will reveal your areas of good and bad body language for children.

The easiest way to illustrate vocal tonality is similar to the way a boss talks to an employee and vice versa. A boss can be very nice to employees, but when they speak it's with a sharper, direct, and confident tone of voice. Speaking to your son without conviction when giving commands is a mistake because when you want a child to do something, they expect you to lead them. Your tone of voice used for normal conversations and commands should be distinctly different. Your child needs to know when you mean business. For example, most parents who are naturally good at vocal tonality will use challenging phrases such as, "excuse me" or "who are you talking to" when their son is disrespectful. Using that type of tone is a warning itself. When you give your commands, record how you sound. Do you sound decisive and confident when attempting to get your son to listen to directions? Are you hopeful? Or are you worried about triggering them? I can always tell a parent who is great with their children simply based on the vocal tonality they use when speaking with their kids. It fluctuates at the perfect moments and changes depending on the circumstances.

Eye contact is looking another person (or animal) in the eye. We all know this one but let's take a look at why it's so powerful. Some parents possess a superpower called "the look". "The look" is that level of communication where an adult gives one glance and that is all it takes to get a child moving (or to stop moving). This pillar of compliance is the one where you're promised to be able to get boys to listen to you without speaking even one word! Eye contact helps because it is an act of challenging your child similar to the "excuse me" response in vocal tonality. If used correctly, it quickly sends a signal to him that this is a warning before consequences are given.

It was always pretty funny when I would work with a child and did not have to say anything to them all day. The teachers would look at me as if I was not doing my job because I did not talk much. However, I was just doing my job at an exceptional level to the point where words were no longer needed. My child and I had an understanding after a few weeks together. He would look at me when he knew he was pushing the boundaries of acceptable behavior. Once our eyes met, he knew exactly what to do, which was to stop or correct his behaviors. It even got to the point where he would over-communicate to ensure that I approved of his actions. It's time for you to be able to simply look at your child when they are acting up and watch as they quickly rethink their behavior because they know *you* mean business. Play around with eye contact and respect it's magic. It's absolutely magnificent how much the eyes can do the talking for you.

A simple way to get started is to look at your son for a few extra seconds without saying much. You can make silly faces or be serious. Kids welcome eye contact (and light staring) whereas most adults find it offensive and threatening. This is due to the fact that kids are pure and enjoy attention whereas most adults hate when people look at them because they think you're judging them or discovering their insecurities. Kids do not have that problem. They may be shy, but they are not insecure. They are free. They do not care about eye contact unless they did something wrong. Have you ever saw a child stare a stranger down in public? It's the funniest thing in the world. The person becomes awkward, uneasy, or gives that fake smile if they are uncomfortable with kids. The child is communicating without saying any words because that's what they love to do. The eyes speak for themselves.

Lastly, when giving interventions or talking in general with your son, always make them look you in the eye because it makes them more likely to comprehend the lessons you are giving. Most boys try to avoid eye contact when they are embarrassed or when they have committed a wrongful act. When they look into your eyes, it forces them to address the situation compared to letting their mind wander off when they are not giving the eye contact.

Chapter 6: Connecting the Dots

How to Avoid Triggers with Boys

If there's one piece of advice you can take away from this section, it's that less is more. Particularly when a child is losing their grip on their behavior and self-control, it's extremely important for you, the adult, the parent, the teacher, to stay calm. In these moments, most people feel a need to gain control of the situation immediately. They feel eyes staring at them. They see their child struggling and they try to react quickly. They argue, try to restrain, or try to give consequences so darn fast that they literally add fuel to the fire. The boy throws a chair, the adult yells. That's one reaction to another. They storm out of the room. The adult chases them. There's another. They say no, you say yes. It's all a chain reaction. The correct approach is to let their fire fizzle out before you intervene. Now, there's going to be situations that require immediate action such as when a child is physically harming another. However, even that situation can be handled with control on your part. No one is going to ask you to be perfect here. Emotions get going and sometimes it's our natural reflex to say, "yes you will" when a child says "no". But the principles still remain. Never ague. If you catch yourself about to argue, stop and say, "okay". Trust yourself to follow through with whatever you said was going to happen. For example:

You: "Xavier, clean that mess off the table before you leave"

Xavier: "Nah I'll get it later; I want to play"

You: "Get it now please"

Xavier: "No"

You: "Yes or else you're not going to play with your friends later outside. Your choice"

Xavier: "Leave me the hell alone, I don't care about the mess, I said I'm going to get it later"

You: "Okay" (in the "okay if that's how you want to play it" tone of voice)

Now if you were to try to "win" this situation, Xavier would have continued to argue or begin other forms of defiant behavior because you're doing what...adding fuel to the fire. Instead, by saying okay, you left the ball in his court. He's going to make the right decision which is to clean up or it's now your job to follow through with the consequence. Over time, if you follow through with consequences, he'll start making better decisions. He'll start walking away, but then turn around and do as you asked because he knows he does not want that problem later. If he makes the right decision, happily (not sarcastically) say, "there's a big boy move, thank you for making the right decision. I'm proud of you". Less was more in this situation. You saved time, effort, and stress by calmly standing your ground and using the correct tone of voice.

Boys who have behavioral disorders such as oppositional defiant disorder and conduct disorder despise authority. The first word of the disorder, "oppositional" means that he is likely to oppose you. If you stand on one side, he'll go to the other. If you try to stop him, he continues. If you tell him yes, he says no. Other kids say, "yay", he says, "boo". The list goes on and on. The best way to avoid triggers is to move with rather than against your child. For example, a boy, age 10, named Jimmy, loved to play sports and videogames. So, when it was time to do any kind of focused work, he would elope to his playroom and shoot around on his mini basketball court. If you go into Jimmy's room demanding he get back to work, threatening with countdowns and rushing him, he would instantly be triggered. Instead, what you should do is calmly stand by for a few seconds and have a little fun with Jimmy. Shoot around with him or just talk about something other than what he expects you to talk about (which is him doing his work). At first, try throwing little bargains in there such as, "okay nice shot, one more and then let's get back". Sometimes Jimmy will complain or sternly say, "no, I don't want to". Your next response would be, "yeah that work is annoying, boring, and sometimes hard. The only thing is...if you stay here and play, you won't be able to play later, and the work will still be there. It's your choice but I'd hate for you to lose that time later. So how about we take one more shot, then go back." Then, Jimmy would take about three more shots to still feel like he's in power and be "defiant" to shooting only once. However, he'll ultimately make the right decision, take a deep breath and return to work. You reward him by helping him out and giving plenty of positive reinforcement on the first few problems or during the whole time if you have it.

All in all, you steer that train you call your son rather than trying to press the brakes. You set up tracks for the train to guide it in the right direction. If you try to stop it, catastrophes happen. You do this by following the sequence above. The first thing is to agree; "...yeah that work is annoying, boring, and sometimes hard...". Second, reshape his perspective; "...The only thing is...if you stay here and play, you won't be able to play later, and the work will still be there...". Third, give him the power to make his own decisions; "...It's your choice but I'd hate for you to lose that time later...". Finally, lead by offering a simple solution; "...So how about we take one more shot, then go back...". Move *with* Jimmy rather than against Jimmy.

You do not always have to help him or reinforce his behavior immediately in that case. This is due to the fact that defiant boys find it insulting or embarrassing when you compliment their good behavior. In their heads, they take your positive attention as an insult because it feels like you don't trust them to make good decisions, whereas they believe they have enough self-control to make the right choices...just when they want to. In other words, here's the thoughts running through their heads: "He would not react excitedly to a good child who listens, so he must think I'm a bad child". "If she's making it such a big deal that I listened, she must think I'm bad. Fine if she thinks that, I'll just keep acting bad since she doesn't believe I can ever be good". You have to be careful with your praise sometimes due to these reasons. This is why we discussed being non-reactive throughout this book. If you stay calm and praise him, he won't have those thoughts. Moral of the story don't get too high or too low on any behaviors your son is showing. There are rare moments where you get compliance and you want to simply leave it be without adding any extra attention to it.

Another great way to avoid triggers is using positive statements rather than negative commands. I observed a parent tell her son to use nice hands instead of saying, "no hitting" so I approached her and asked her how much those two phrases work in comparison. Unfortunately, she was unaware that she even used such a positive command. She was surprised that anyone noticed her parenting style. She thought her style was what everyone else did. This is a very common occurrence. Not me approaching parents asking them about their strategies and methods, but it's rather common for parents to be unaware, whether good or bad, about their habits. If no one points out our habits, it's hard to notice them. It's rare to find a parent who takes deliberate actions and strategies to enforce discipline, communicate effectively, and create harmonious relationships with their kids. On the other hand, there's millions of parents who wing it and are either naturally good or bad which is largely based on how they were raised. That's why you're an above average parent. You take action to become better.

Using phrases such as "nice hands" was a true eye opener. Once again, we're trying to avoid triggering that oppositional part of the brain. The best way to do that is to encourage, suggest, imply, and guide your son. "Nice hands" has a positive effect on the psyche as it's not even a command. It's just a statement that implies a certain action or correction. Some other examples of positive statements include "breathe" instead of "calm down", "big boys act this way" instead of "you can't act this way", and "because you will be healthier and make more friends" instead of "because I said so". These sequences, examples and positive statements will help you avoid triggering your son if he has oppositional behavior disorders.

Following Through, Meaning What You Say

A parent's ability to give consequences and follow through determines how seriously their son will take them. There must be actions behind your words. Too many parents talk a big game, but never follow through. This is the main reason why their sons remain non-compliant. Parents will complain for days about their son's behavior, but when I ask, "What did you do about it" and hear a bunch of excuses, I know exactly the type of parent I'm dealing with...an undisciplined parent who expects their young child to be disciplined.

Has your child ever told you that they don't care about their punishment earlier in the day when you want them to do something, but later in the day when it's playtime, they get apologetic and sorrowful about their earlier decision? If you let them get away with this, you just got played for a sucker. For example, let's say Jordan is acting crazy and wild in the store. He's completely freaking out when you tell him he can't have this toy, that juice, or those snacks. Instead of feeding into his behavior, you take the correct action of staying calm and telling him he will not be able to play with his toys when you guys get home if he continues. However, after about ten more minutes of complaining and falling out on the floor, he finally calms down and is very pleasant the rest of the way. Because of this, you decide to forget about the punishment because Jordan looks sad. In this situation, it's usually the wrong decision to let him have a pass. Why? Well, his behavior continued for ten minutes after you told him his consequence. That's unacceptable if you want long term results. Due to that, regardless of how well he is currently behaving, Jordan would still owe me time. It would not be a large amount of time unless the behavior went overboard. However, that determination is up to your discretion. During his timeout, you should describe to him what he did, ask why he felt that way, explain what he did wrong, and how he is supposed to act in that situation in the future to avoid receiving this consequence again. The only way the punishment would be considered a pass is if he immediately stopped his behavior after the initial warning was given. You can also pass on the punishment if Jordan has been showing improvement. For example, if he used to yell, hit, and cry when he did not get his way, but this time he only cried, I would tell him that he did a much better job handling himself, so he does not have a punishment. Or, if this is the first time in three months he has lost control compared to his history of losing control every week. Focus on severity and frequency of behaviors to establish your son's rate of improvement. Give consequences accordingly.

When following through, the child may not be consciously trying to trick their parents, but their natural instincts tell them to do whatever it takes to play that videogame or to play with their toys. They completely forget that they were misbehaving just a few hours ago. If parents back down because they feel bad, they're scared to trigger him again, or they're simply too lazy to give out the consequences they said they would give, how does that make them seem? Well, let's take a look at the descriptions above. "They back down", "they're scared", and "they're lazy" are all signs of one thing...weakness. A child senses that lack of a backbone and will never follow the directions of a weak leader.

Be careful. One time a parent asked, "do you think a good punishment would be for me to give my son a wacky haircut to teach him a lesson". I told this parent to rethink the word punishment. Sure, that punishment may embarrass your son and make his mistake very memorable which could deter him from ever doing it again. However, let's double down on our punishments by making them positive. I recommended that this parent make his son write a positive, one-page letter to someone he knows every day for one week. That's a valuable punishment. A bad haircut only influences him to avoid bad behaviors whereas complimenting other people influenced him to act on positive intentions. You double down on consequences by replacing them with positive actions rather than just trying to stop the negative ones.

Be sure to follow through with your consequences. Nothing changes if you don't mean what you say. Lastly, timeouts are the best moments to give lectures because that's usually when he wants out of the situation. He will listen to whatever you have to say in this moment because you have leverage on his privilege of free time. During timeouts, always recap what he should do the next time to avoid a timeout and make him verbally repeat what you said. You could also use writing assignments where your son must repeatedly write out an affirmation. For example, "I will listen to adults the first time. If I listen the first time, I won't get in trouble. I won't get in trouble because I am a good kid. If I'm a good kid, good things will happen to me".

The Power of Bonding

The use of small challenges as well as coaching your son while he overcomes his fears is a skill employed by the best parents in the world. Now before you lose your mind and say, "what the heck, I don't know how to challenge my son or help him overcome his fears properly", don't worry, that's fine. The good news is that these challenges can be simple and small. The bad news...well there really isn't any. The only difficult part about this tactic is knowing *when* to use it. For instance, let's say you buy your family a bunch of sandwiches from the deli one night for dinner. You have two sons and two daughters. Everyone in the family except your son with behavioral issues likes the works on their sandwiches. The like lettuce, tomatoes, bacon, sweet peppers, mayo, chips and everything else. You son with poor discipline likes his food to be quite simple. He just wants turkey and cheese. His sandwich is going to be lighter than everyone else's right? Well, normally you give out the sandwiches to everyone because they're wrapped with writing on it. Your son isn't at the age where he can identify the written ingredients on a sandwich. In a scenario such as this one, you can challenge your son to figure out which one belongs to him before he opens it. Why? You're teaching him to use his brain to figure things out for himself, which of course, increases his confidence and his independence. He probably will be confused and ask for help, which is fine. You still want to challenge him to figure it out on his own and encourage him to make mistakes. Then, guide him to choosing the correct sandwich by asking, "how do we figure this out". You're now challenging him to be a leader and problem solver. Next you'd say, "well this one is pretty light. What do you think that means?". Then eventually you keep asking these questions step by step until he realizes which sandwich is his. We just turned the simplest situation into a life lesson of leadership, problem solving, independence and resiliency. That right there is an all-world parent who is teaching their son how to be self-sufficient in multiple areas.

What about fear? Well if your son is afraid of the dark, put him on a mission to find his favorite toy in the dark. We want to leverage his fears against his desires to see which one is more powerful. Be there to guide him, but don't hold his hand. His desire for pleasure will eventually overpower his irrational fears, especially with your support and encouragement. He'll see that fear is not always bad and he should feel comfortable attacking his fears rather than running away from them. People read and repost motivational quotes all the time that say, "don't let fear hold you back", but how many of those people actually live by the words, take those actions, and teach others. I trust you're one of the people who do take the action because you're reading this book. Challenging your son and guiding him through his fears and mistakes leads to an inseparable bond. You might be wondering, "what does this have to do with my son's behavior"? That's what you're about to find out.

Bonding is the establishment of a relationship or link with someone based on shared feelings, interests, or experiences. The key term in that definition is "shared feelings and experiences". People to whom we relate hold our ears, eyes, and attention compared to those who do not. That's why you are reading this right now. We share a bond. A bond of dealing with difficult children. You must find where you and your child can relate to one another in order to get compliance. From a logical standpoint, you are their parent. You feed, clothe, and provide shelter. Logically, the child knows they need you to survive. However, when you take the time to build a bond, the child will crave your approval as emotional support as well. Remember how we discussed leverage previously? Well, with a strong bond, leverage can be as easy as not giving your child attention. Losing your warm, fun, engaging, caring love can be enough of a deterrent against their poor decision making. It's essential for parents to understand that they must address each child specifically and give the child what they need rather than what the parents want to give. There is a difference.

Some children have very nice, sweet parents. But, if those parents are also passive, we have a problem. Most defiant children do not respond well to passive people. They see these people who do not have "edginess" or a strong sense of personal boundaries as being weak, particularly if they can cause reactiveness in that person. For example, if a person hears a comment and the expression on their face along with the tone of their voice shows that the comment shocked them, then that person is an easy target for a defiant child. Reactiveness shows a weaker frame of mind which we discussed earlier in the second chapter. Boys with behavioral issues respond to authority figures who are very compassionate, but who also establish clear expectations. People who have compassion, but firm expectations usually have a strong sense of self control and empathy for others. They likely have a higher level of social intelligence as well. All of those traits are aligned with the mindset needed to reshape and guide boy behaviors. When the child who struggles with behaviors loses their control, they need a strong figure who will be non-reactive to be able to trust that person.

On the other hand, some children have very aggressive, authoritarian, "my way or the highway" type of parents. Those parents are too far on the other side of the spectrum. No defiant child (or any child) needs someone yelling and barking orders at them all day. They need someone who will talk and listen to their viewpoint. It's important to switch between these roles depending on what the child needs from situation to situation. In a co-parenting household, you may both alternate roles from time to time as well (i.e. good cop bad cop strategy), but if you are both very aggressive or too passive with your child, it's going to be ineffective with boys. As a single parent, do not feel discouraged. None of the children I have worked with required me to have a partner in the field when delivering services which means you can play both roles when necessary as well.

Fun is the most vital tool in your arsenal when it comes to bonding with your son. Be silly. They say, "girls just want to have fun". Well, guess what? Boys just want to have fun too. Sharing that side of yourself with him keeps you feeling young as well. Stop being Batman all the time and start taking some notes from the Joker. To this day, the simplest reason why I am so great with kids is because I enjoy acting like one when the time is right. Crack some jokes, play sports, share stories, dance, smile, and laugh with them. Tell them they are good. Tell them you're proud. Tell them they're the greatest. All of those things are important with these boys because sometimes all they need is for someone else to believe in them. It can really be that simple. If you're told you are a bad little boy all day, then that's the way you're going to act. It becomes the affirmation of your personal identity. If you're told and more importantly, taught that you can be the best, it has the same effect, just in a positive way.

Build a strong bond with your son and you'll begin to find out that the simple chance of you not giving him attention is all you need to get compliance. This particularly became evident during a few cases where the child would ask me not to leave them at their school. Their tone of voice was not sad. They spoke it in a way that said, "aw man, I was having fun with you and you understand me. Don't leave." It was hard for me to leave those kids but as a parent, you don't have to worry about that because your child is with you forever. When boys feel like they are being good for your approval, this adds a whole new level of compliance because you don't have to do much to keep them in line. They begin to follow directions naturally. This is the sweet spot. Building rapport and a connection trumps all other pillars because once you have that bond, it does all the work for your relationship.

The Art of Interventions

You have the power to teach your child how to manage their triggers. If your son is struggling, one intervention is all that is necessary to change his behavior for the rest of his life. I'll prove it to you. In this section we will go over a few examples that reveal some ways to properly teach your son how to heal his emotional and behavioral disturbances on his own.

One evening, you and your son decide to go grocery shopping for the night after you pick him up from school. The two of you are casually walking down the aisles in the store. Uh oh, here comes the toy aisle. You know what's coming:

Him: "Mommy, can I have this toy (that costs $79.99)"

You: "No son, we just came here for some quick groceries, I'll get it for you some other time"

Him: "But I want it now"

You: "Come on, let's go"

Him: "No"

You: "I don't have time for this today please, let's go"

Then all hell breaks loose. He starts destroying, yelling, falling, crying, kicking, and everything else. What do you do? Next up is the 4-step intervention plan I have used for this situation and countless others while working with these boys. Use it, tweak it if you must, and watch your son learn to manage his emotions and behaviors. Let this serve as your long-term plan to reshape any behavior you want as it encompasses the best methods of communication, discipline and development. Let's get to it.

Step 1.a: Move to a place where extra attention is not present

If your son is defiant, but calm enough to have a conversation, calmly try to influence him to move to a place where extra attention from other people is not present. Extra eyes make the situation 10 times worse because then he may try putting on a show. At times boys will walk or run away to a secluded place anyways so it works just fine. Just follow him calmly until he stops. The best thing you can say to him if he keeps running is that you can do this all day (even if you can't).

Step 1.b: Back off and wait patiently

If he is still losing control to the point where he will not talk (such as the yelling, falling, crying, kicking, and everything else part), back off and wait patiently. Do not speak initially. Hold off for a few seconds and let him calm himself first. If you try to talk right away or make any moves, it can further the aggravation as it builds pressure. However, if you wait for him to calm himself, it can throw him off and make him wonder why you aren't saying anything. This makes him open up for your attention rather than trying to fight against it. He becomes sad instead of angry. He'll then feel like you're with him instead of against him. In a nutshell, it opens the lane for communication.

- Pro Tip: Never react! Never react! Never react! Holding your composure is the #1 rule. Your level of steadiness should be as if they are simply reading a book or at the playground (basically as if they are doing normal activities)

- Pro Tip: Also, your proximity should be close. The farther away you are, the louder you have to speak, and it makes the situation more threatening. Reduce your height to the child's level to be eye to eye or get close to their ear. Proximity makes the situation more direct and allows you to lower your tone which naturally signals compassion for the child. This makes you more influential and allows your son to save face from any kind of embarrassment

Step 2: Engage in conversation

Engage in conversation at a calm tone. Keep your tone, voice, and emotions at a steady level. Never argue. If he starts talking back or losing control again, try step 1 again. Never blame your boy during an intervention. This does not mean you cannot say he was wrong. It should just be framed in a question rather than a statement. If you believe he was wrong by his actions (which is more often the case than not), the best way to disagree with what he did is to ask him, "what do you believe you could have done to avoid getting in trouble or getting upset". He'll likely respond by saying "I don't know" or blame someone else, but that's fine. That's a completely different message than "that was wrong, you shouldn't have done that". Words such as those will trigger his oppositionality. A question such as "what could you have done" is deeper psychology where you are inferring that he is in control of his outcomes and actions. Boys with behavioral problems need to know that they are in control of their actions and outcomes because most believe that the world is against them and there is "nothing they can do" to control it. This is where remorseful victimhood plays a role. You want to weed that out as much as possible or the behaviors will continue.

- Pro Tip: Breathing is extremely effective in getting your son to calm down. Breathing is something we can all control, so it brings a sense of relief. If your child won't calm down, encourage them to breathe before trying step 2

Step 3: Empathize, don't sympathize

Sympathy is not empathy. Sympathy means to feel pity for another. Pity is reserved for those who are helpless in a situation. Yes, your son is struggling, but he is not helpless or hopeless. Giving sympathy breeds excuses and excuses never get you closer to results. Instead, be empathetic. You show that you can relate, but that you also expect improvement. How do you do this? Tell a similar or embarrassing story of yours. Laugh at your ridiculous stupidity and pain while explaining what you would have done to handle the situation better. Let's say the child was called "stupid" by his peer or sibling and that set him off. Ask him if he actually believes he is "stupid". Give him an example of a time where his smarts were prominently featured to disprove any self-esteem doubts he may have. Now you're building confidence in your child. Now his emotions and perspective should take a turn for the positive at this point.

Step 4: Plan for the future

Together the two of you come up with a solution for how you will handle a similar situation the next time. Do not let him leave until he can look you in the eyes and verbally repeat the solution you came up with. You may even act it out with role playing depending on how much his mood has changed. However, sometimes he does not want to talk after he has calmed down so you can let him go for a bit. Nevertheless, once you see that his mood is happy or positive again, that's when you call him over to speak about the lessons for future situations similar to the one that triggered him. If he still does not want to talk about it, then you have to risk triggering him again by shutting down his fun until you get through your expectations for future instances. You really should get that lesson through his head sooner rather later to teach him how to manage his emotions and behaviors on his own. Otherwise the behaviors will continue. The more time that passes, the less he will remember what happened especially with emotions running so high.

That is the short-term intervention plan to handle each situation. This last section is a true, brilliant story that teaches you how to get long term results with one intervention.

One day, a single mother around the age of 32 had a question about her son, age of 6. She wanted to know why her son was having meltdowns in school and during his extracurricular activities when she was not there. She said that when she took the right steps of asking him what was he feeling in those moments and tried to understand him, all he could verbalize was that his brain told him to do things like yell, be extremely defiant, kick chairs, make noise and bother classmates. Teachers and staff would try to get him to calm down, but nothing would work. Mom was afraid that her son's behavior would worsen. Luckily, her son was always remorseful for his actions. So, after getting to know their relationship a little better by asking a few questions, we both agreed that her son had a healthy level of fear towards his mother. This was a good thing. It meant that he would never act this way in front of her because he knew there would be consequences. It was evident to me that he enjoyed releasing his pent-up aggression when she was not around. He would cry when she would show up to the school to pick him up. It wasn't because she was going to beat him. It was just that he knew she would take away his free time and be put on boring punishment when they got home. She followed through with consequences. One thing she did incorrectly was yell at him about his behavior before trying to understand. This may not have been the best initial approach but once again, no one is perfect, not even a parent who loves their child. Ultimately, she was confused about what to do. Her son showed signs of autism and now he was showing signs of behavioral issues as well. It was clear that her son needed an intervention. But I wasn't going to be the one to do it. She was. I told her that next time he had this same sort of situation, to give me a call. Now usually, I would give pre-planned action steps to help in this situation, whether it's referring her to a private provider or giving her some quick tips to rethink the way she handles him. But, because this particular situation did not involve her son misbehaving in *her* presence, she did not need either of those solutions just yet. I tried a different approach because he was an "out-of-home" defiant boy.

There are "out-of-home", "in-home", and kids who show behavioral issues in both settings. The out-of-home boys are the ones who, as you can see, misbehave only when they are not around their primary caregiver (or someone who has a close relationship with the primary caregiver such as friends and family). The in-home boys are the ones who show behavioral issues at the home only when they are around their primary caregiver, relatives, friends, and their immediate family. The boys who are both will act up with and around anyone. And of course, there are inverses or gray areas such as kids who act up at home based on the learned behaviors from a terrible school. In this case, it's an inverse or gray area because the school won't tell the parent about their kid's bad behaviors if every child is acting the same way in that school. Vice versa, a parent won't tell the school about their child's behavior if they don't consider the behavior to be a problem at home. Whoever allows the negative behaviors in either situation is the enabler. Whoever is traumatized and struggles to manage the child is the receiver. Simply due to the fact that the enabler does not know or does not care about the negative behaviors enough to report them, it leaves the receiver confused about where and why the child has this behavior. Ultimately, the child is bringing acceptable negative behaviors from one setting to a setting where those same negative behaviors are unacceptable.

Let's finish the story. So, this young mom and her young son had an issue of behavior. He exhibited out-of-home behavioral issues. The next time he got in trouble at school, the mom did what she was told and called me. She was a bit late because she had already yelled at him again on the way home from picking him up. However, we still were in the perfect spot. He was crying when they got home, she sent him to his room and that's when she called. Of course, she was a bit frustrated and worked up, but here is exactly what I told her to do in one intervention that changed her son's behavior forever.

Mom walked into her son's room. He sat up. She did not say anything. She let him cry and let the silence fill the room. No tv, no music, no one else. It was just her and him sitting there while he calmed down and wondered what was going on. After about five minutes of silence she broke it by calmly asking, "so, what happened today, why are we here?". He did not answer at first. He was searching for the right words to say. She waited for about a minute and then said, "your teacher said you could not follow directions and did not listen. You began to hit classmates and throw things. So, why did you feel that way, what made you do that? (Side note: her voice was compassionate as she sought to understand. I don't usually have these conversations this way. I have a relaxed tone that implies "this is no big deal, you're free to tell me what happened so we can solve the problem". I'm giving you this side note so you know to use either tone in this example or use one that fits your personality naturally. The main principle is to stay calm, but firm). Her son said, "I don't know, my brain told me to". She said, "okay does it go blank and then you can't think?". He shook his head yes. After his mom asked questions and summarized what he said, he feels understood. She calmly told him to come close and stand in front of her. She told him to give her a long hug. Then she said, "whenever you feel that way, we're going to do this instead" (this is the point where I switch to a compassionate tone). She told him that he was to breathe deeply, and she made him do that about five times consecutively before continuing. She finished by telling him that he was strong and a good boy. She made him verbalize that statement out loud about five times while positively reinforcing him after each time with a smile and a soft, "good". She ended the intervention by asking him, "who is strong and good". He responded saying, "I am". Mom said, "why". Her son finished by saying, "because I am in control".

This is why we said the healthy level of fear he has for his mom is good. That fear comes from her ability to follow through consequences which makes giving interventions easy because her son is going to be compliant to avoid making his consequences worse. This situation is very intimate and powerful for their relationship. The tactics used such as breathing and affirmations are small. It's the overall atmosphere of the situation that I told her to create - that's what made it powerful. Staying silent at first was done on purpose. Telling him to come close and to give her a calm hug in silence was deliberate as well. Everything was patient and very slow. These types of minor tricks make the intervention more dramatic and the more dramatic it is, the more memorable it will be for the child. Ultimately, he was given a replacement solution for when he feels as if he is losing control and needs to calm himself before his brain goes "blank". The mother did not question how he felt or what he said to try to *fix* her son. She just summarized and confirmed what he felt in order to understand him. He was still on punishment thereafter, but the intervention was so powerful that her son remembered what she taught him without any further practice for months. He went from having days of severe, untamable behavioral issues at school three times a month to having those issues relapse only once every 6 months. She was surprised at how much he remembered what she taught him without ever doing it again. He would say, "remember how you taught me to breathe mommy, I did that today". He started being more confident and positive because she told him he was strong and in control. Her little guy even started using the same solution from the intervention anytime he got frustrated with homework. And finally, her days were much easier and stress-free knowing her son was self-regulating his own emotional, mental, and behavioral state.

Some parents believe that these tips, trainings, and methods must be the most complex solutions in the world. They think reshaping behaviors involves a 20-page step-by-step document or formula. No. They key is the little things you do. Interventions are simple, but dynamic. It's about being strong and calm with your son. It's about asking questions, then creating positive solutions to replace negative behaviors rather than judging and trying to give answers.

Conclusion

So, here we are. You have it. All of you mothers, fathers, teachers, providers, and specialists know the why, the what and the how to manage boys with behavioral problems and a lack of discipline. If your son is violent, you know how to use leverage. If your son is attention seeking, you know when and when not to ignore him. If your son has a negative perception, you have the power to change his mindset. When he gets out of control, you know how to bring him back to a state of peace. When he tries to argue, you know to stop talking and to simply follow through. But most of all, if your relationship within your family was hurting, you now have the knowledge to heal. And if you still need extra help, you know where to go.

Take this final opportunity to join the Kidshapers Family (www.facebook.com/weshapekids) – an online community designed for parents just like you. Use the experiences, failures, and successes of people who have been in your shoes. There's no better and healthier way to make sure you get through this battle without losing a piece of your soul. If our support is not enough, we will take it upon us to refer you to a provider who can meet your needs. It's all about awareness, ending cycles of negative behaviors, and forecasting a positive future. It's our only goal by any means necessary. Thank you. If you enjoyed this book, please spread the word with a review by clicking HERE (https://www.amazon.com/dp/B084VTDC2L).

Printed in Great Britain
by Amazon

57915580R00063